ESSEX BUSES

JOHN LAW

AMBERLEY

First published 2017

Amberley Publishing
The Hill, Stroud
Gloucestershire, GL5 4EP

www.amberley-books.com

Copyright © John Law, 2017

The right of John Law to be identified as
the Author of this work has been asserted in
accordance with the Copyrights, Designs and
Patents Act 1988.

ISBN 978 1 4456 6178 0 (print)
ISBN 978 1 4456 6179 7 (ebook)

British Library Cataloguing in Publication Data.
A catalogue record for this book is available from
the British Library.

Origination by Amberley Publishing.
Printed in the UK.

Introduction

Essex is one of England's most varied counties. Part of it was placed within Greater London during the 1974 boundary changes. Ilford, Upminster and Romford became part of the capital; however, other towns such as Loughton and Epping, served by both red London buses and the Underground network, are part of the capital's sphere of influence but have remained outside of County Hall's clutches.

South Essex, alongside the Thames, is very much an industrial area, with the docks of Tilbury, cement quarries around Grays and oil refineries at Thames Haven and Canvey Island. Beyond these is the resort of Southend-on-Sea.

The rest of Essex is very rural – surprisingly so in view of its closeness to London. Small towns like Maldon and Ongar still feel very remote. Nevertheless, there are several large towns and one city. Colchester, dating back to beyond Roman times, is Britain's oldest town, while the county's administrative centre, Chelmsford, was recently given city status. Clacton-on-Sea is the largest of several seaside towns and ports.

The major bus operator in Essex was, until recently, Eastern National. This company, dating from the early years of the twentieth century, grew from a steam bus manufacturer – the National Steam Bus Company – after that concern decided to expand into bus operation. Services started in London, but they soon took over the bus routes previously operated by the Great Eastern Railway around Chelmsford.

National, as the company was then known, rapidly expanded, serving London and Hertfordshire, before moving outwards to the West Country. Retrenchment began in the 1929, when London General took over the services in Hertfordshire and South Bedfordshire. Meanwhile, in 1928, the major four railway companies had acquired an interest in National. The business was split into four, with Eastern National being formed in 1929. Originally, Eastern National was responsible for the operations of the National Midland area, though that was later to become United Counties in 1952.

Meanwhile, the formation of the London Transport Passenger Board in 1933 meant that the services in East London and around Grays were transferred to that company. The Thomas Tilling Ltd organisation gained a controlling interest in Eastern National in 1931. That business also owned Westcliff-on-Sea Motor Services, which then became a subsidiary of Eastern National, not being completely absorbed until 1955. Various independents were also taken over by Eastern National, with names like Hicks and Moore Brothers vanishing into history.

Like all the former Tilling operators, Eastern National was taken into the National Bus Company in 1969. NBC green replaced the similar green colours of the previous owners. Then came Margaret Thatcher's government, with a policy of privatisation. Eastern National adopted a yellow-and-green livery, prior to being subject to a management buyout. Then, in 1990, the company was sold to Badgerline, who split the business into two. The southern part of the company became Thamesway, adopting a yellow-and-maroon colour scheme. Firstbus became the owner of both companies following the merger of Badgerline with GRT Holdings. First Essex became the fleet name and, gradually, the corporate colours were introduced to the streets of Essex.

In the west of the county, London Country was the dominant operator, running the majority of services around the Grays and Harlow area, with depots in both towns. Upon that business being split up, London Country North East took over, later to become County Bus & Coach in Essex and part of Hertfordshire. In 1994 County was sold to West Midlands Travel, but was passed on to the Cowie Group soon afterwards. Cowie later metamorphosised to become Arriva; they are still the main operator in Harlow, though most of the Thameside services have passed on to other concerns.

The two municipal bus operations in Essex – Southend-on-Sea and Colchester – are also now in the hands of Arriva, though those in Colchester are operated by a subsidiary, TGM, trading as Network Colchester.

Perhaps, in the world of buses, Essex is best known for its independents. One of the largest of them was Hedingham and District, based at Sible Hedingham in the Colne Valley, near Halstead. This operator gradually expanded, taking over various other independents, including Osborne's of Tollesbury and Went's of Boxted, as well as Suffolk-based businesses Partridge of Hadleigh and Norfolk's of Nayland. Hedingham Omnibuses, as the company is now known, became part of the Go-Ahead Group in 2012 and is retained as a separate entity. From its original area, operations have expanded into the Tendring Peninsula around Clacton-on-Sea.

Another bus company taken over by the Go-Ahead Group in 2012 was Chambers Coaches, based at Bures, a village straddling the Essex/Suffolk border. Operating a fleet of red buses, Chambers ran the long Colchester–Bury St Edmunds service, via Sudbury, which was a journey of around two hours. Because the founders of the company were devout Methodists, no Sunday services were operated – a situation still in place today. Like Hedingham Omnibuses, Chambers Coaches retains its identity, though under the management of the former.

Other pre-deregulation independents included Ward's of Epping, with a local service to Coopersale, and Lodge's of High Easter, who still run an occasional bus into Chelmsford. More small operators included Channel Coachways, serving Southend Airport; Viceroy of Saffron Walden (with a fascinating fleet); and Ford's of Althorne, near Burnham-on-Crouch.

After 1986, various independents commenced running bus routes in Essex. One of the largest of these was Harris Bus of Grays, running many services around that town. The company went into liquidation in 1999, with the area later becoming the territory of Imperial Buses, Ensign and others.

The Colchester area also saw an expansion of services by independent companies. Carter's (based in Suffolk) and Cedric's of Wivenhoe were later to be taken over by New Horizon Travel, who no longer run significant stage-carriage services.

Chelmsford, once the centre of Eastern National operations, now sees buses from Regal Busways and Stephenson's. The latter also now has operations around Southend and Bury St Edmunds (Suffolk).

There are, of course, many companies that do not operate stage services, instead concentrating on contract and school duties. One of the largest was S&M/Castlepoint Bus Company, based around the South Essex industrial area. Others include Wiffen's of Finchingfield and Boon's of Boreham.

All of the above operators are to be seen within these pages, providing great coverage of the county's buses since I started visiting the area in the early 1970s. As well as my own photographs, I have included a few from my Essex-based friend, Richard Huggins, to whom I am most grateful. I must also thank the owners of Bus Lists on the Web, who have saved me hours of trawling through various books while writing the captions for this publication. In addition, I must also express my appreciation to Jim Sambrooks for proofreading this book and supplying additional information.

Part of the western extremities of Essex fell under the domain of the London Transport Executive. The pleasant village of Abridge was long served by AEC RT types. Number RT2880 (MLL 627) in the fleet was found in the village, awaiting departure beside the Blue Boar pub *c.* 1975. The vehicle is a Park Royal-bodied bus, built in 1952.

Loughton is one of the towns that, in reality, is part of the Greater London conurbation, but comes under Essex for administrative purposes. London Transport number RF427 (MXX 404), a standard AEC Regal IV of 1953 vintage with a Metro-Cammell forty-one-seat body, is seen on Roding Road, Loughton, in 1973.

Harlow New Town was constructed to house Londoners displaced by the devastation of the Second World War. A spacious bus station was built to serve the adjacent town centre. Here, in 1974, is London Country's RT3816 (NXP 823), an AEC Regent III, with fifty-six-seat Weymann bodywork – one of many such vehicles inherited from London Transport in 1970.

Another vehicle that was transferred to London County in 1970 was RF253 (MLL 790), a thirty-nine-seat AEC Regal IV/ Metro-Cammell intended for Green Line duties. Seen in London Country's version of that colour scheme, the bus had been relegated to local bus duties when photographed in Harlow bus station in 1974.

In 1974, when this photograph at Harlow's bus station was taken, London Country had begun a modernisation programme to replace the aging ex-London Transport buses. A batch of Leyland Atlanteans was received in 1972 and one of these, numbered AN80 (JPL 180K), is pictured here in its pre-National Bus Company colours. It is, for the technically minded, a PDR1A/1 Special with seventy-two-seat Park Royal dual-door bodywork. This had an o.680 engine and spring parking brakes – standard on the AN68 model, but not on PDR types. The flat fare of just six new pence seems very reasonable for a local journey within the town.

A special vehicle in the London Country fleet was this Ford Transit with a Dormobile sixteen-seat body, delivered in 1974 for the Harlow 'Pick-Me-Up' dial-a-ride service. Number FT5 (XPE 125N) is seen at Harlow bus station in 1975 outside Zelley's Jewellers – a firm still trading today.

The area around Grays and Tilbury was also served by London Country buses, from a depot (though LCBS always called it a garage) in the former town. Based at that location was number RCL2239 (CUV 239C), an ex-London Transport AEC Routemaster with Park Royal sixty-five-seat bodywork, fitted with platform doors for use on Green Line duties. It is seen in 1976, towards the end of its life and downgraded to bus duties at Tilbury Riverside railway station. Train services from here finished in 1992, but the ferry from Gravesend still operates.

Unlike the majority of National Bus Company operators, London Country did not really take to the Bristol VR type of double-deck bus. However, a small batch was delivered to Grays Garage. Numbers BT13 and BT15 (PPH 473/5R), both VRT/SL3/501 types with seventy-four-seat single-door ECW bodies, are seen inside their home in 1977, only a few months after being delivered. Both buses were disposed of to the Bristol Omnibus Company in 1980.

Though most of Essex was Eastern National territory, fellow National Bus Company operator Eastern Counties ran routes into the county. In the north of Essex, close to the border with Cambridgeshire, is the delightful little town of Saffron Walden. Here, on 14 January 1974, Eastern Counties number LM627 (FAH 627C), a 1965-built Bristol MW5G with forty-five-seat bus bodywork, is seen ready to depart for Cambridge. Back then, the single fare for the whole journey would have set one back all of nineteen pence!

The red buses of Eastern Counties also served Colchester, running in from Ipswich (Suffolk). At Colchester's bus station, in March 1993, is number VR188 (PVF 360R). This Bristol VRT/SL3/6LXB, with standard ECW bodywork and a capacity for seventy-four passengers, is painted in the latest post-National Bus Company livery of the time. That colour scheme would soon be replaced by First Group's 'Barbie' stripes, while the multistorey car park forming the backdrop to the photograph was destined to be demolished.

The Eastern National Omnibus Company (ENOC) was by far the largest operator of buses in Essex. By the early 1970s, the business had passed from the British Transport Commission to the National Bus Company. Therefore a very much standard Bristol/ECW fleet of vehicles was employed. A good example is seen here in Southend-on-Sea, *c.* 1974. Number 1301 (1863 F) is a 1958-built Bristol MW5G with forty-five-seat ECW bodywork, still in its post-NBC colours, albeit with the newer fleet name.

Eastern National's number 1441 (NWC 15) is seen here in Braintree in the mid-1970s. It was new in 1963 to Tilling, ENOC's coaching subsidiary, as a thirty-nine-seat coach. This Bristol MW6G/ECW combination is shown in NBC green bus livery, as it had been converted to bus duties and fitted with less luxurious seats. Alongside is more modern Bristol RELL6G/ECW bus number 154 (RPU 882K).

The 1970s double-deck Eastern National fleet also consisted mainly of the Bristol/ECW combination. Number 2497 (1842 F) is a typical example. This Bristol LD6B Lodekka was new to the company as number 1528 in 1957, with a seating capacity of sixty passengers. It is seen in central Southend-on-Sea sometime around 1973/4.

Later Lodekka deliveries to Eastern National consisted of the longer FLF6G type. Three are photographed here at Hadleigh depot, near Southend, in 1980. From left to right, they are 2943 (AVW 402F), 2900 (WVX 527F) and 2907 (WVX 524F). All carry standard ECW bodywork, though 2943 was delivered new with coach seating for the express service to London; it is shown here after it had been downgraded to bus duties.

Being a resort town, Southend-on-Sea naturally had open-top buses for the numerous day trippers. Still in service as late as 1976 is number 2383 (WNO 479), a 1953-built Bristol KSW5G. It was new to ENOC's subsidiary, Westcliff-on-Sea, and originally had a 'lowbridge' ECW body, seating fifty-five. The bus has a good load of sun-worshippers on board as it runs along the Promenade and passes the famous pier.

Like many fellow National Bus Company fleets, Eastern National took delivery of many Bristol VR-type double-deckers. Number 3048 (JNO 189N) was very much a standard VRT/SL6G, built in 1975 with ECW seventy-seat bodywork. In 1980, it was repainted in this special version of the original ENOC livery to celebrate fifty years of the company's existence. The bus is seen in that year when departing from Southend's bus station for Chelmsford.

The Leyland National became the obligatory single-deck bus throughout most of the country's NBC fleets. Eastern National was no exception. Forty-nine-seated example number 1875 (BNO 665T) is seen in close company with two sister buses, awaiting their next duties in Southend-on-Sea in late 1980.

Delivery of ENOC's Bristol VR double-deckers continued into the 1980s. New in November 1980 was number 3083 (STW 27W), a VRT/SL3/6LXB with ECW seventy-seat bodywork. It was photographed, still in full NBC colours, on a rail replacement service at Ingatestone station on 26 October 1986. I am grateful to Richard Huggins for supplying this photograph.

Although it was ordered by Southdown, this 1981-built Bristol VRT/SL3/6LXB was delivered to Eastern National as number 3118 (XHK 223X). Carrying a seventy-four-seat ECW body, it was photographed by Richard Huggins as it departed from Halstead's small bus station on 25 February 1984.

In a break from tradition, Eastern National received a small batch of lightweight Ford R1014 vehicles with Duple Dominant bus bodies, seating forty-three passengers. Based in the Hertfordshire town of Bishop's Stortford, this example, number 1002 (MAR 777P), is seen at Chelmsford bus station, Essex, in 1981.

Another unusual vehicle for a National Bus Company fleet was Eastern National number 1110 (HHJ 371Y), one of a batch of Leyland Tigers with Alexander TE-style coachwork. Painted in National Express white livery, this fifty-three-seat coach is photographed in spring 1985 when leaving Colchester for Clacton. The multistorey car park over the bus station has since been demolished.

Chelmsford bus station has also seen considerable change since this photograph was taken in 1981. Eastern National's driver training vehicle LFS 289F, allocated fleet number 9017, is a former Eastern Scottish Bristol VRT/LL6G, bodied by ECW. The Bristol VR marque did not find favour north of the border, and several NBC concerns received batches of them in exchange for older Bristol FLF types.

Like many companies at the time, the late 1980s saw an influx of minibuses to the Eastern National fleet. Typical was number 0218 (C218 HJN), a Mercedes L608D/Reeve Burgess twenty-seater. It is seen in Clacton-on-Sea bus station in spring 1989.

Eastern National's Bishop's Stortford depot received a small batch of unusual Bedford YMQS buses such as this example, number 1050 (TJN 973W). Carrying Wadham Stringer dual-purpose thirty-three-seat bodywork, it was photographed by Richard Huggins on 16 October 1986 at its terminus, Bardfield End Green, Essex.

Eastern National's post-NBC livery style is displayed to good effect on Leyland National bus number 1921 (JHJ 147V), a forty-nine-seater built in 1979. Richard Huggins photographed it outside Bradwell nuclear power station on a sunny New Year's Eve in 1987.

The Leyland Lynx was introduced as a replacement for the earlier Leyland National. One of Eastern National's examples is seen in Ingatestone Market Place, on 10 August 1989, through the lens of Richard Huggins's camera. Number 1429 (F429 MJN) is a standard example of the batch, capable of seating forty-nine passengers.

The winter sun was shining on Braintree's small bus station parking area when Richard Huggins visited on 27 December 1991. Posed nicely were Eastern National numbers 1310 and 1309 (ANA 94Y and ANA 93Y). These ECW coach-bodied Leyland Leopards had been new to National Travel West, but look very smart in their new paintwork.

Another second-hand vehicle in the Eastern National fleet, number 3218 (ONH 924V) is seen arriving at Colchester's bus station in the summer of 1991. This Bristol VRT/SL3/6LXB with ECW seventy-four-seat bodywork had been new to United Counties in 1980, when it carried fleet number 924.

Eastern National number 3230 (SUB 789W) also started life with another operator. It was new to West Yorkshire Road Car Company as number 1765 in 1981. In its smart green-and-yellow livery, it is seen on the corner of High Street and Market Hill in Maldon on 24 February 1996. (Richard Huggins)

At first glance, this is just a Peugeot 505 estate car. However, it was licensed as a seven-seater bus and was used by Eastern National for its Countrycar services. Given ENOC fleet number 0120, B258 CHK was actually owned by Braintree District Council. According to the relevant leaflet of the time, 'The service operates different routes each day from Tuesdays to Saturdays amongst many small villages providing off peak access to facilities in the towns of Braintree, Witham, Halstead or Sudbury.' It is seen in Braintree in the summer of 1993. The services were to be withdrawn a year later.

It is a beautiful summer's day in Southend-on-Sea on 13 August 1989, and Eastern National 3501 (NPU 974M) has attracted a few brave passengers. Delivered new in 1973 as fleet number 3027, this Bristol VRT/SL6G originally had a seventy-seat standard ECW body, complete with roof. (Richard Huggins)

This coach-seated Leyland Olympian was quite a rare beast, as very few were built in this style. Eastern National number 4512 (D512 PPU) was new in 1986 and carried ECW coachwork, seating seventy-three passengers in relative comfort. Intended for commuter routes to London, the bus is seen on a less prestigious working, having come into Colchester bus station on the 53 route from Chelmsford. At one time, service 53 was Britain's longest bus route, running from Tilbury Ferry to Harwich – a distance of 85 miles. Alternate buses also ran to Clacton-on-Sea. By the time this photograph was taken in March 1998, the service had been cut back to terminate at Colchester.

In 1990, Eastern National became part of the Badgerline group – hence the badger taking a sniff of the rear wheels of bus number 640 (K640 GVX) as the vehicle is made ready for service in Chelmsford depot in spring 1994. Typical of the larger minibuses of the time, it is a Mercedes 709D with twenty-three-seat Plaxton bodywork.

In 1995, Badgerline merged with GRT Group to become Firstbus, and the now familiar 'F' logo began to appear on Eastern National buses. Here is such an example, seen in Colchester bus station (after the demolition of the multistorey car park above) in March 1997. Number 1507 (P507 MNO) is a Dennis Lance with Northern Counties forty-nine-seat bodywork, almost new at the time.

Labelled as the 'Stansted Connection', First Eastern National Mercedes 709D/Reeve Burgess twenty-three-seater number 2609 (H609 OVW) is seen heading for Bishop's Stortford in February 2001. The location is on the High Street in the pretty Essex town of Saffron Walden, at the junction with George Street.

When Eastern National became part of the Badgerline organisation, the company was split into two operations. The area of South Essex, featuring such towns as Southend-on-Sea, Basildon and Grays, became the territory of Thamesway. Transferred in from the main Badgerline fleet is number 716 (C510 BFB), still in its Bristol area livery, but lettered as a Thamesway bus. This Ford Transit sixteen-seater is seen in Southend-on-Sea in 1991. Minibuses of this size would soon prove inadequate and would be replaced by larger Mercedes vehicles.

The later style of Ford Transit minibus, seen in Thamesway colours at Southend-on-Sea's central bus station in April 1991. New in October 1986, number 0756 (D756 OWC) has a sixteen-seat Dormobile body.

At the same location as the above photograph, and on the same day, we see Thamesway number 349 (H359 LJN), a twenty-three-seat Mercedes 709D, bodied by Reeve Burgess. It was new to the company in 1991.

Resplendent in the new Thamesway livery is number 1907 (DAR 129T), seen approaching Southend-on-Sea's central bus station on a market day in April 1991. This forty-nine-seat Leyland National had been new to Eastern National in 1979.

Like its sister company, Thamesway became part of First Group in 1995. The logos of that business are clearly visible on P707 HPU – unlike the fleet number! It had been delivered new in 1996 as number 707. The bus is a Dennis Dart SLF with Plaxton thirty-seven-seat bus bodywork. It seen in Basildon bus station in February 1997.

First Group soon began painting its buses into its 'Barbie' colour scheme, starting with new low-floor buses, but soon the rest of the fleets followed. New in March 1998 was First Thamesway number 719 (R719 DJN), a Dennis Dart SLF with thirty-seven-seat Plaxton bodywork. It is seen, when almost brand new, at Southend's central bus station.

First Group later adopted a five-digit national number scheme. The use of local fleet names was also abandoned. This policy made transfers within the group much easier. Fleet number 34286 (P186 TGD) started life with Strathclyde as number VO86 in 1996, but is seen in Harwich on 8 March 2008. The bus is a Volvo Olympian, bodied by Alexander. To its right is the High Lighthouse, built in 1818. It ceased to function in 1863 and has recently been restored.

Due to its closeness to Greater London, Brentwood has long been a 'border town', where London's red buses met those of the provincial operators. Ex-Eastern National Leyland Olympian C407 HJN, delivered in green in 1986, was originally numbered 4007. It is seen on Brentwood High Street on 5 June 2009 in First's standard colours, with fleet number 34807. Unusually, this ECW-bodied bus has seventy-two high-backed dual-purpose seats.

Duke Street in Chelmsford town centre is the location of this photograph, taken on 10 May 2007. Since then, Chelmsford has been given city status. Firstbus number 46813 (L813 OPU) is a 1994-built Dennis Dart with Plaxton Pointer thirty-four-seat bodywork.

Firstbus number 32818 (T818 LLC) was new to Capital Citybus in London, but is seen in later life outside Grays railway station, in First's 'Barbie' colours, on 1 July 2014. Originally dual-doored, this Plaxton-bodied Dennis Trident has been converted to one-door operation, as this nearside view clearly shows.

Another bus that started life with Capital Citybus was Firstbus 41005 (R705 VLA). This East Lancs-bodied Dennis Dart SLF thirty-seven-seater is seen in Southend-on-Sea, 24 February 2011, when about to depart for Hullbridge. This journey will take it northward through Rochford and towards the estuary of the River Crouch.

Transfers within the First Group to the Essex operations were quite common. Fleet number 47221 (M221 VWW) was built for Yorkshire Rider in 1995. This Alexander Dash-bodied Dennis Dart was capable of seating forty passengers. On 9 May 2007 there was adequate capacity for the shoppers of Braintree as it loads up in the town's small bus station.

Sister bus to the one shown above, number 47252 (M450 VWW) looks beautiful in the old Eastern National colours as it passes Chelmsford bus station on 10 May 2007. First Group has done a similar job on other buses throughout its organisation, bringing back memories of liveries long vanished.

Duke Street Bridge, passing under the Great Eastern main railway line and part of Chelmsford station, is negotiable only by single-deck buses. Firstbus number 67007 (P507 MNO) has successfully passed through unscathed, and is about to enter Chelmsford bus station. New to Eastern National in 1997 as number 1507, this Dennis Lance has forty-nine-seat Northern Counties bodywork. Passengers on board gasping for a pint will be disappointed to see that The Original Plough has yet to open its doors; nevertheless, the Railway pub just the other side of the bridge will, no doubt, quench their thirsts.

Firstbus number 43856 (EG52 FGD) is one of four Dennis Dart SLF buses purchased for operations around the Clacton-on-Sea area. All had started life in 2002 with Connex, where they had served the Channel Island of Jersey. Originally registered J101726, the bus has a Caetano body with a capacity of twenty-nine-seated passengers. It was photographed in central Clacton on 24 October 2013.

Stansted Airport, close to the Hertfordshire border but located in Essex, attracts buses from around both counties. Firstbus operate the X30 Aircoach, running between Southend-on-Sea and the airport terminal. Seen on such duties is 20805 (YN08 OWV), departing from Chelmsford's bus station on 27 January 2010. This forty-four-seat coach has Plaxton bodywork on a Volvo B9R chassis. Meanwhile, No. 90026 departs from the adjacent railway station on the rear of a Norwich-bound express.

At one time, the X30 service was operated by smaller vehicles such as 56004 (EY54 BPX). This is an unusual Mercedes Vario with Plaxton Cheetah coachwork. It is seen in Duke Street, Chelmsford, on 10 May 2007, pursued by a more conventional Optare Solo. 56004 has since been transferred to Scotland.

Firstbus, in the Essex area, purchased several Scania CN94UB OmniCity forty-one-seat single-deckers in 2006, for services around Chelmsford. In fleet livery, lettered 'Chelmsford City', number 65032 (YN06 TDZ) is seen having a rest in Chelmsford bus station's parking area on 22 May 2014.

Sister vehicle 65028 (YN06 TDO) is also seen in Chelmsford, in the town centre (Chelmsford did not become a city until 2012), on 10 May 2007. Less than a year old, the bus is painted in an eye-catching black livery, dedicated to Park & Ride duties.

Colchester's 'Jumbo' water tower dominates the background as Firstbus 65690 (YS03 ZKK) passes the town hall on the High Street on 10 May 2007. New to the company's Essex operations in 2003, this single-decker is a Scania L94UB with forty-three-seat Wright bodywork.

Just over a year old when photographed at Duke Street, Chelmsford, on 22 May 2014, is Firstbus number 44357 (YX13 AEF). Dedicated to Chelmsford City services, it is a thirty-nine-seat Alexander Dennis Enviro saloon.

Firstbus number 69913 (BV13 ZBU) is one of several unusual Volvo 7900H integral hybrid single-deckers in the fleet. These forty-seat buses were purchased for the 100 service to Basildon and Lakeside shopping centre. It is pictured as it sets out on its journey from Chelmsford's rebuilt bus station on 22 May 2014.

Transport for London's route 498 runs from Romford into the Essex town of Brentwood. First Group is obliged to use the red livery on its operations in the capital, and number DML 44082 (YX58 HVM) is no exception. This Alexander Dennis Enviro has a dual-doorway layout and can seat twenty-nine passengers. It is seen in Brentwood High Street on 5 June 2009.

Colchester Corporation began tramway services in 1904, but from 1929 only operated motorbuses. By 1974, when this photograph was taken, the fleet consisted mainly of rear-loading Leyland double-deckers. Seen in the depot, on the right is number 33 (MWC 133), a PD2A/31 with sixty-one-seat Massey bodywork. Alongside are AEC Regent V buses 55 and 60, which would soon be withdrawn.

Colchester's fleet began to be updated in the late 1960s, incorporating vehicles such as number 49 (YWC 649F), a 1968-built Leyland Atlantean PDR1/1 with seventy-four-seat Massey bodywork. It is seen, through the lens of Richard Huggins's camera, on 25 February 1984 as it circumnavigates the town's bus station.

Colchester Borough Council continued to order Leyland Atlanteans throughout most of the 1970s. However Massey Brothers had ceased production, and so the products of Eastern Coach Works found favour. This Atlantean AN68/1R, delivered in 1975, has ECW bodywork of a design that was to be found only in Colchester and South Yorkshire. This example, number 58 (JHK 498N), is seen loading up in Colchester bus station in 1980.

A later Leyland Atlantean AN68/1R is seen at the same spot, also in 1980. Number 73 (TPU 73R) was delivered in 1977, with a more conventional style of ECW body, though, like number 58 above, capable of seating seventy-four passengers.

For its single-deck operations, Colchester Borough Council relied on the trusty Bristol RELL6L. This 1973-built example, number 18 (YWC 18L), is seen descending East Hill as it leaves the town centre, *c.* 1979. Fifty-three-seat ECW bodywork is fitted.

Colchester Borough Transport was sold to British Bus in 1993. Four years later, British Bus came into the hands of the Cowie Group. The CBT fleet name and livery were retained and are seen applied to number 352 (NIW 6512), photographed in the town's (now roofless) bus station in March 1997. This bus started life as Crosville number SNL6 (FCA 6X) in 1982, a standard dual-doored Leyland National. It was later rebuilt as a forty-nine-seater single-door bus to the 'Greenway' specification; this was for London Country, another British Bus subsidiary, prior to being transferred to Essex.

Colchester Borough Transport number 30 (H130 LPU) stands in front of one of the most photographed dovecots in the world, as it poses in the parking area of the town's bus station in the summer of 1991. The bus, new to CBT in 1990, is a forty-nine-seat Leyland Lynx 2, an unusual type of vehicle for a council operator.

Colchester Corporation Transport suffered a bus shortage in the early 1970s, and several vehicles were hired in from other operators. In 1974, Southend Corporation's number 206 (2717 HJ) was on loan and is seen here in Colchester High Street. The bus is a 1961-built Leyland Leopard L1 with bodywork by Weymann. A nice Austin van, typical of the period, overtakes, while a Morris Traveller turns left from North Hill.

Another hired vehicle on loan to Colchester Corporation was Great Yarmouth Corporation number 78 (PEX 178K). This AEC Swift has forty-three-seat dual-doorway bodywork by Willowbrook, and is seen in the company of an Eastern National Bristol MW in Colchester bus station in 1974. At least one other municipal operator, Leicester, also helped out by supplying buses during the crisis.

In late 1997, the Colchester Borough Transport and other operations of the Cowie Group were renamed as Arriva. That operation's standard colours were gradually applied, but the Colchester business was then sold to Arriva-owned Tellings-Golden Miller, who rebranded it as Network Colchester. Bearing that operator's colours is number 337 (G617 BPH), a Volvo B10M-50 Citybus with East Lancs bodywork. New to London Country (South West) in 1989, it is seen in Queen Street, Colchester, on 10 May 2007.

New to the Tellings-Golden Miller Group was Network Colchester number 102 (YN06 TFZ), a Scania N94UD with East Lancs eighty-seat bodywork. On 7 May 2007, it was found on rail replacement duties at Colchester's main railway facility, locally known as North station, as it is a good distance from the town centre.

Network Colchester number 310 (N540 TPF) is seen negotiating Queen Street in the town on 10 May 2007. This vehicle, a 1995-built Dennis Dart with East Lancs forty-seat bodywork, was new to London Country as number DS20.

With the rebuilding of Colchester's bus station came a reduction in capacity, so many routes were obliged to avoid it. Doing just that is Network Colchester number 355 (Y50 TGM), a Dennis Dart SLF with distinct Caetano bodywork. As the registration indicates, it was new to TGM for its West London operations. It was photographed on 10 May 2007.

Network Colchester's number 363 (SN54 HXB) is seen in the town's High Street, with the town hall forming the backdrop, on 10 May 2007. This 2004-built Dennis Dart SLF has a thirty-seven-seat 'Pointer'-type body, built by Alexander. Tellings-Golden Miller-owned Burton's Coaches bought it new.

Essex's other municipal operator was Southend Transport, who ran a fleet of blue buses around the North Thameside conurbation. The presence of the former London, Tilbury & Southend Railway necessitated the use of 'lowbridge' buses on certain routes. A typical vehicle in the fleet was number 315 (PHJ 954), a 1958-built Leyland PD3/6 with Massey L35/33R bodywork. It is seen in the depot, *c.* 1975. Hans Ueber, advertising on the bus, was a well-known caterer in the town.

More Massey bodywork is carried on this 1965-built Leyland PD3/6, though to 'highbridge' specification. Seating seventy passengers, number 334 (CJN 434C) was one of a batch of eleven such vehicles. Towards the end of their lives, several were hired out to other operators, including Cardiff City Transport, London Transport and London Country. It is with the latter, still in Essex, that we see 334, operating service 397 in Harlow.

A most unusual vehicle to carry Southend Transport's blue colours was number 317 (KCK 879), a Leyland PD3/4, with Burlingham seventy-two-seat full-fronted bodywork. It was new to Ribble Motor Services in 1958. Three such vehicles were hired from Ensign Bus Company, all of which were painted in Southend livery, though they were only in use for just over a year, before being shipped abroad to Hong Kong. On 3 June 1974, it is seen at the outer terminus of route 1, Rayleigh railway station.

Open-top buses were essential on the seafront service in Southend-on-Sea, as the bridge leading to the pier had very limited clearance. Passengers will have memories of the conductor ensuring that all upper-deck passengers were seated as the bus passed this point. Having safely negotiated the manoeuvre, number 314 (PHJ 953), another Massey-bodied Leyland PD3/6 of 1958 vintage, is seen on Western Esplanade sometime around 1974.

Southend Corporation Transport purchased a batch of ten Albion Lowlanders in 1963. The last of these was withdrawn in 1977, but number 332 (7096 HJ) was removed from the fleet in the previous year. It is seen, departing from the depot, only a few months before its demise. Seventy-seat Alexander bodywork was carried.

The Southend fleet was not entirely double-deck. In the town's suburbs we see Leyland Leopard number 209 (GJN 509D), heading for 'Eastwood–Belgrave Road', situated just off the famous Southend Arterial Road, close to Leigh-on-Sea. New in 1966, the bodywork was constructed by Marshall, to dual-doorway layout, seating forty-nine passengers.

A further batch of Leyland Leopard saloons was delivered to Southend in 1968, this time having fifty-one-seat dual-doorway bodywork by East Lancs. Number 216 (MJN 216F) is seen close to the town's central bus station in 1980, with a light load for Eastwood on route 6.

Despite the Bolton registration, LBN 201P was new to Southend Transport as fleet number 201. One of two such coaches delivered in 1976, it is a Leyland Leopard with Plaxton Elite Express coachwork, seating fifty-one passengers. It is seen inside the depot when almost brand new. Sister vehicle 202 still survives today, ferrying passengers around Knebworth Park.

By far the largest batch of vehicles purchased by Southend Transport consisted of forty-eight Daimler Fleetlines, bodied by Northern Counties, with dual-doorway layout and seventy seats. Delivery began in 1971 and the last one was received in 1976. Number 350 (WJN 350J) was one of the earlier vehicles and is seen at the central bus station in late 1980.

More Fleetlines joined the Southend Transport fleet in 1979 and 1981, built by Leyland. Number 241 (MRJ 241W), again with a Northern Counties seventy-seat body, was one of the last to be delivered. It is seen close to the town centre in autumn 1983.

A visit to Southend's depot in 1986 revealed a most unusual vehicle on hire; Leicester City Transport number 14 (PJF 14R). This Leyland Leopard, with Willowbrook 'Spacecar' coachwork, seating fifty-three passengers, is lettered as a Gibson Division coach. Gibson Brothers once ran a Leicester–Market Bosworth service, before the business was sold to Leicester City Transport in 1979.

Southend Transport was not immune to the 1980s craze for minibuses. Number 402 (E402 BHK) was a twenty-five-seat Optare City Pacer, based on a Volkswagen LT55 chassis. New in 1987, it is seen in the spring of the following year in Southend's central bus station.

Deregulation saw Southend Transport greatly increase its coach fleet, mainly for use on express services towards the capital. With its destination blind displaying 'London', number 205 (BTE 205V) is probably on a schools duty, as it was photographed by Richard Huggins at Fambridge railway station on 3 March 1986. New in 1980, the vehicle is a Leyland Leopard with Duple Dominant fifty-one-seat coachwork. Folding doors are fitted, making it suitable to be used on normal stage services.

New to Southend Transport in 1976, number 905 (JTD 395P) was originally a Northern Counties-bodied Daimler Fleetline, with dual-doorway. It was later converted to be open-top, as seen in this photograph in the town centre in April 1991. Given the expected weather in that month, it is rather surprising that the bus is being used on a normal bus service!

Like many operators at the time, Southend Transport saw that competition might have been deterred by the introduction of withdrawn AEC Routemasters from London Buses. Here, in April 1991, number 121 (CUV 256C) arrives in the town centre. It still carries its original fleet number, RCL2256, indicating that it is a 30-foot version of the marque, unlike many others purchased by Southend, which were standard 27-foot examples.

High-backed dual-purpose seats are clearly fitted to Southend Transport number 265 (H265 GEV). This Leyland Olympian has a Leyland-built body, capable of carrying seventy-four seated passengers. It is seen on the same occasion and at the same place as the Routemaster above.

Southend Transport was sold to the British Bus Group in 1993, which was later taken over by the Cowie Group. A rebranding exercise saw Cowie become Arriva, today a part of the Deutsche Bahn empire. On 24 February 2011, a reminder of British Bus days is seen in central Southend-on-Sea, albeit in Arriva colours. Fleet number 3021 (N221 TPK) was new in 1996 to British Bus subsidiary London Country, as number LS21. It is a Dennis Lance with East Lancs forty-nine-seat bodywork.

New to Arriva's Southend operations was number 4258 (KX13 AVE), an Optare Versa integral forty-four-seat saloon. Less than a year old when photographed on 3 January 2014, it is seen on Chichester Road on the fringes of the town centre.

Originally new to Arriva's Medway Towns operations in 2013, number 4224 (GN62 HMY) soon crossed the Thames for use in Southend. On 3 January 2014, this Wright Streetlite DF thirty-seven-seater is seen in central Southend, at the southern end of Chichester Road, loading up on route 1 to Shoeburyness.

As well as operating in Colchester and Southend, Arriva also have pockets of territory around the fringes of East London and the industrial part of Essex along the north banks of the Thames estuary. In red for its operations in the capital, Arriva London's ART3509 (KE51 PUV) is about to depart from its Grays terminus for Romford. The latter town is today in Greater London, but Grays is still firmly in Essex. This Wright-bodied DAF saloon, fitted with dual-doors and thirty-one seats, was photographed on 17 February 2007.

Arriva inherited services around Grays when Cowie took over County Bus, which was once part of the Blazefield Group. The company's operating area extended up to Harlow and a small part of eastern Hertfordshire. One of Arriva's most prestigious services is the 510 route between Harlow and Stansted Airport. Operating this route on 28 April 2007 is 3857 (KE54 LPC), a Volvo B7RLE with forty-three-seat Wright bodywork, seen in Harlow bus station.

Arriva also operate Green Line route 724, running between Harlow and Heathrow Airport, via Hertford, St Albans and Watford. A small fleet of dual-purpose Mercedes-Benz O530 saloons is dedicated to the service, having thirty-nine seats and painted in an appropriate livery. Fleet number 3907 (BU06 HSL) is seen leaving Harlow bus station on 8 August 2012. The journey to Heathrow will take over three hours.

County Bus, in Harlow, used the name 'TownLink' for its local services in the Harlow area. Carrying such branding is this Volkswagen LT55/Optare City Pacer twenty-five seater E521 PWR. Note that County did not use fleet numbers. The bus had been new to Welwyn Hatfield Line in 1987 and had been inherited when that company sold out to the Blazefield Group in 1990. It is seen in Harlow bus station in February 1993.

County's F786 JKX, a 1988-built Iveco 49.10, is seen at Harlow Town railway station on an evening in January 1990. The twenty-one-seat minibus has bodywork by Reeve-Burgess. It was new to London Country (North East) as fleet number MB796.

Arriva's Harlow operation was, for a few years, branded as Network Harlow, as part of the associated TGM Group. Bearing the livery of the time is number 3257 (V257 HBH), a Volvo B6BLE with Wright forty-seat bodywork. The vehicle is seen approaching Harlow bus station on 8 August 2012.

Not yet painted into Network Harlow livery is HX04 HUH, a Dennis Dart SLF bodied by Caetano, with twenty-nine seats. It was new in 2004 to Linkline of Harlesden, London. As it approaches Harlow bus station on 8 August 2012, it does not carry a fleet number. The bus was later transferred to Colchester, where it became 1564.

Deregulation and privatisation in the mid-1980s saw some strange things happening in Britain's bus industry. One of the most bizarre was former National Bus Company-owned East Midland Motor Services starting up operations in East London and West Essex. On 7 March 1987, Mansfield & District (a trading name of East Midland) number 42 (A42 XHE) is seen beside Blackmore Pond, about 3 miles from the small town of Chipping Ongar. The vehicle is a 1984-built Leyland Tiger coach, bodied by Alexander with forty-nine seats. (Richard Huggins)

We are looking north along Chipping Ongar's High Street on 17 April 1988. Heading south is East Midland number 503 (HCA 976N), an ex-Crosville Leyland National forty-eight-seat dual-purpose vehicle. The company's foray into Eastern National territory did not last long. East Midland later became part of the Stagecoach Group. (Richard Huggins)

The massive Lakeside shopping centre opened in 1990 on the site of an old quarry. Situated close to Grays and Thurrock, it is very well served by buses from all directions. Looking very much like a rural scene, Stagecoach East London number 19790 (LX11 BHF) is actually about to enter the sizeable bus station at Lakeside on 1 July 2014. This Alexander Dennis Enviro double-decker will soon return to Hornchurch, within Greater London, on route 372.

The town of Loughton is thought by many to be part of the capital, as it is served by red buses and the London Underground. Nevertheless, it is situated firmly beyond the boundary and is definitely in Essex. However, here is a bus that has clearly come out of London. Docklands Transit was founded by Harry Blundred (of Devon General fame) in 1988, but it later became Docklands Buses when in the hands of the Go-Ahead Group. On 17 March 2007, Dennis Dart SLF/Caetano saloon HV02 PCO is seen outside Loughton station, about to return to Ilford.

Essex was once graced by several notable independent bus companies; ranking as one of the most loved of these was Osborne's, who were based in the historical village of Tollesbury, close to the mouth of the River Blackwater. A regular service was operated into Colchester, where fleet number 18 (8071 ML) is seen in 1974. New as an AEC demonstrator in 1962, this AEC Renown with Park Royal bodywork operated for London Transport for some time, prior to sale to Osborne's in 1962. It later passed into preservation.

Number 35 (JEV 706N) in the Osborne's fleet was new to the company in 1975. This Bedford YRT/Willowbrook fifty-five-seater bus is loading up for Colchester in its home village of Tollesbury, despite the destination blind reading 'Private'. In addition to the Colchester run, Osborne's also operated a regular service to Witham railway station.

Number 29 in the Osborne's fleet was also new as a demonstration vehicle. This Bristol VRSL6G, registered GGM 431D, had a longitudinal engine, hence the 'VRL'. After its early career it went to the Bristol Omnibus Company, where it was given fleet number C5000. The ECW-bodied bus is seen with Osborne's in Colchester bus station in 1978, alongside number 22 (FWC 392H), a Bedford VAM70 with forty-five-seat Duple Viceroy coachwork.

Given fleet number 1 in the Osborne's fleet was JKE 341E, an ex-Maidstone Borough Transport Leyland Atlantean PDR1/1 with Massey seventy-two-seat bodywork. After a hard day's work, this fine vehicle has just returned to the depot one evening in the spring of 1980. In 1997, Osborne's of Tollesbury was taken over by another Essex independent, Hedingham Omnibuses.

Hedingham Omnibuses was once one of the largest independent bus companies in Essex. A red-and-cream livery was employed, as seen on fleet number L200 (J295 TWK), a fifty-one-seat Leyland Lynx 2 that was new as a demonstrator in 1992. The bus is seen during March 1993 in Sible Hedingham High Street, a few hundred yards from the company's headquarters.

The 'L' prefix to Hedingham Omnibuses' fleet numbers dates back to 1960, when Mr McGregor purchased the business of Letch of Sible Hedingham to form Hedingham & District (as it was then known). Number L198 (K198 EVW) was purchased new in 1992 and is a Dennis Dart/ Alexander Dash forty-three-seater. It is seen in the summer sun at Colchester bus station in 1995.

Number L366 (S127 ELR) in the Hedingham fleet is a Volvo Olympian with Alexander R-type bodywork. It was new to Metroline in London in 1998, but is seen here in Colchester at the corner of High Street and North Hill on 13 October 2011.

Another second-hand bus in the Hedingham fleet, L354 (M604 TTV) is seen in Colchester town centre on 10 May 2007. New to Nottingham City Transport in 1995, this Volvo B10B-58 saloon has Alexander Strider fifty-one-seat bodywork.

More Alexander Dash bodywork is seen on Hedingham Omnibuses L303 (L67 UNG), but the chassis this time is a Volvo B6-50. New to Ambassador Travel of Norfolk in 1994, the forty-one-seater is seen negotiating Queen Street in Colchester on 10 May 2007.

Not all of the Hedingham fleet was second-hand. A new purchase in 2005 was number L340 (EU05 CLJ), a Wright-bodied Volvo B7RLE. This forty-four-seat saloon is seen in Halstead High Street on 9 May 2007.

Another modern bus on the books of Hedingham Omnibuses was number L355 (EU07 GVY), an Alexander Dennis Enviro 'decker; it was brand new when photographed in Halstead on 9 May 2007. Five years later, in 2012, Hedingham Omnibuses became part of the Go-Ahead Group and, at the time of writing, has been retained as a separate entity.

In 1991 Hedingham Omnibuses took over a Suffolk independent, Norfolk's of Nayland. Much of that company's stage-carriage work brought their buses into Essex. Arriving in Colchester in the mid 1970s is 759 KFC, a 1960-built AEC Reliance/Park Royal forty-four-seat saloon, new to City of Oxford.

Seen laying over at Colchester bus station in 1978 is SBN 767, belonging to Norfolk's of Nayland. This 1961-built AEC Regent V/MCW double-decker had been purchased from Greater Manchester PTE in 1976, but had originally been new to Bolton Corporation as fleet number 167.

Another small independent, Went's of Boxted, ran a service from Colchester to the company's home village, about 5 miles away to the north. Commencing in 1927, the route was served by Went's until 1991, when the proprietor took retirement. Peeping out of the depths of Colchester bus station in 1976 is 47 UNU, a Bedford SB1 of 1961, with Yeates forty-one-seat coachwork. It had been new to a Derbyshire operator, Felix of Stanley.

At Went's operating base, a field in Boxted, in spring 1980 are LGV 994 and YTA 268. The coaches are Duple-bodied Bedford SB3s. LGV originally started life with Burton's of Haverhill in 1958, while YTA had been new to Thrathen of Yelverton, Devon, in the same year. Both forty-one seaters saw regular service on the route to Colchester.

At Colchester bus station in the spring of 1985 is VPX 640K, a Seddon Pennine 6 coach, bodied by Plaxton in 1972, when it was new to an operator in Haslemere, Surrey. It is seen here in the hands of Rules Coaches, from Boxford, Suffolk, from whence it had arrived on service. It is parked next to Went's-owned Bedford/Willowbrook saloon SCP 344N.

The village of Bures sits atop the border of Essex and Suffolk, and was home to Chambers Coaches. The business could trace its history back to 1877, when the founders were strict Methodists, so no Sunday services were operated during the years of independence. The company's main route was from Colchester to Sudbury and Bury St Edmunds. In spring 1989, departing on its two-hour run on the 223 is F243 RRT, a Leyland Olympian with Alexander eighty-one-seat bodywork; it was almost new when photographed.

Approaching Colchester bus station on 10 May 2007 is Chambers's S848 DGX, a Volvo Olympian/East Lancs 'decker. It had been new to Metrobus, an operator from South London, Surrey and Sussex, in 1998. Five years after the photograph was taken, Chambers became part of the Go-Ahead Group; it retained its livery and identity, but was managed as part of the Hedingham business.

Beestons, an independent based in Hadleigh, Suffolk, run several services in and around the company's home town. Their vehicles are often to be found in Ipswich but, in the 1990s, the operating area extended into Essex and Colchester in particular. In March 1993, Leyland National bus PJI 5914 is seen departing from the bus station, heading to Bury St Edmunds. Re-registration makes tracing a vehicle's history a nightmare, but this bus is believed to have been new to Merseyside PTE as fleet number 1872 (RKA 872T).

Carters Coach Services is another Suffolk bus operator, with its headquarters in Ipswich. Today, Ipswich Borough Transport owns the company but, when this photograph was taken in summer 1991, the business was truly independent. Several stage-carriage services in North East Essex were and still are operated, taking passengers into Colchester. Number 877 (XPW 877X) is seen arriving in that town's bus station. New to Eastern Counties, the vehicle is a coach-seated Leyland Leopard with ECW bodywork, originally seating forty-seven passengers.

Another Carters Coach Services-owned bus – this time in a green livery – is seen arriving in Colchester bus station in 1994. UNW 928R is a Bristol VRT/SL3/6LXB with ECW seventy-four-seat bodywork, new to West Riding as number 784 in 1977. As can be seen, not all the vehicles carried fleet numbers.

Looking smart in its red-and-yellow colours is Carters number 456 (R156 LHK). This double-decker had been new to Dublin Bus as number RV388 (98-D-20388) and is a Volvo Olympian with Alexander bodywork. It is seen close to Colchester Castle in the town centre on 13 October 2011.

After deregulation, Cedric's Coaches of Wivenhoe began operating services into Colchester, serving the town and the area around the River Colne estuary. At the depot in 1991 is NCD 563M. This Bristol VRT/SL6G with ECW seventy-two-seat bodywork had been new to Southdown as fleet number 563 in 1974.

Given fleet number 24 by Cedric's, B109 LPH is a more unusual vehicle than the regular Bristol VRs or other buses used on the stage services. New to London Country as LRC9 in 1985, this coach-seated Leyland Olympian, bodied by ECW, had been intended for Green Line duties into the capital. In mid-1998 it is seen while still being used on semi-fast duties; it is about to depart from Colchester bus station on the 78X to Brightlingsea. In April 2013 New Horizon Travel purchased the Cedric's Coaches business.

Althorne is a rural village close to the estuary of the River Crouch. It is home to Fords Coaches, who have been operating excursions, schools duties and the occasional bit of stage-carriage work since the 1920s. A variety of double-deckers was once owned, including 819 HNO, a 1956-built Bristol LD6B with standard ECW sixty-seat bodywork. It was new to Eastern National as number 1502. It is seen in the depot yard, *c.* 1975, in the company of a Dennis Loline and an AEC Bridgemaster.

West's Coaches of Woodford, just into Essex from East London, once operated the service from Loughton to Epping and Ongar. Seen in February 1998 at Loughton railway station (on the London Underground) is NFN 70M, an ex-East Kent forty-nine-seat Leyland National. The 201 service had been transferred to West's Coaches in 1986 from London Transport.

G. F. Ward's depot in Epping was always worth a visit, as can be seen from this photograph taken there in 1973. On the left is an ex-City of Oxford AEC Bridgemaster, 306 MFC. In the centre we see SOU 451, a Dennis Loline purchased from Aldershot & District. Finally, to the right is PFN 877, a former East Kent AEC Regent V with Park Royal fully fronted bodywork. These buses were used mainly on schools duties, but Ward's also operated the 381 Epping Green–Coopersale bus route.

On a cold wintry day in early 1978, another visit to Ward's depot yard revealed three more vehicles. The most interesting, perhaps, is the one on the left, registered 9962 SF. This AEC Bridgemaster/Park Royal bus had been new to Scottish Omnibuses as fleet number BB962 in 1963. Also seen are GJN 423N and PPE 673R, both Ford R1114 types, though with differing styles of Plaxton bodywork. G. F. Ward had purchased both coaches new.

Harris of Grays was a long-established coach operator, who diversified into stage-carriage work soon after deregulation in 1986. Several Essex County Council-tendered routes were won and the company also ran some commercial services. New to Harris Bus in 1986 was D30 PEV, a Volvo B10M-46 with Plaxton thirty-five-seat bodywork. It is seen in the company of a London Country Leyland National at the old bus station in Grays in the spring of 1988.

Loading up in Grays bus station on a foul day in late 1989 is E309 HPU. Harris Bus had purchased this unusual bus new in the previous year. It is a Leyland Swift with thirty-seven-seat Wadham Stringer bodywork. Behind are two County Bus-owned buses lettered for 'Thameside' duties, a Leyland National to the fore and a Leyland Lynx at the rear.

When Lakeside shopping centre fully opened in 1990, Harris Bus began running regular services to serve its customers. At the bus station there is PBD 41R, operating the Car Park service in summer 1991. This is a former Northampton Transport Bristol VRT/SL3/6LXB with Alexander seventy-two-seat dual-door bodywork. A sister bus is seen behind. Harris Bus eventually purchased seven of this type of vehicle, though one was only as a source of spares.

As well as being a well-known dealer, Ensignbus run several services in South Essex. At Grays on 17 February 2007 is number 640 (G740 RTY), a DAF SB220, built in 1989 with an Optare Delta forty-nine-seat body. It had been new to Northern General as fleet number 4740.

Pictured is another sunny day in Grays, on 1 July 2014, as Ensignbus 784 (784 EYB) passes the town's railway station. That particular registration had previously been used on various vehicles in the past and, no doubt, is being used on another bus or coach as you read this. In May 2015, number 784 reverted to its original identity as HV52 WTJ. The Caetano-bodied Dennis Dart SLF had been new as a dual-doored bus with Mitcham Belle, who had used it on tendered London services. It was converted to single-door layout when it was in the hands of Countryliner in Sussex. After service with Ensign, the bus passed to another Essex operator, Trustybus.

At the same spot as the above photograph, but on 17 February 2007, is Ensignbus 703 (P503 MOT). This is another Dennis Dart SLF, but the bodywork was built by UVG, from Waterlooville in Hampshire. This style of bus body later became the Caetano Compass, which was superceded by the Caetano Nimbus, like the one at the top of the page. P503 MOT had been new to a Heathrow Airport operator in 1997. Ensignbus sold the vehicle in 2009 to Arriva, for use in the North Midlands area.

Ensignbus route X80 connects two railway stations with two shopping centres. It runs from the Bluewater complex in Kent, serves Greenhithe station, uses the Dartford Crossing, and then goes to Lakeside and finally Chafford Hundred railway station in Essex. That is where we see number 126 (PO58 KPT) on 1 July 2014. This Volvo B9TL with Optare eighty-one-seat bodywork had been new to Kent County Council, who had used it on Park & Ride duties in Canterbury.

The hybrid bus has come to Essex! Ensignbus number 501 (EU62 BSV) is arriving at Lakeside bus station on 1 July 2014. New to the company, it is a Volvo B5LH with Wright Gemini 2 bodywork and a capacity of eighty-one seated passengers. It is lettered as 'Thurrock's First Electric Hybrid Buses' for the 'Electric Blue 22' service, which operates between Grays and Aveley.

Number 785 in the Ensignbus fleet, registered AE55 EHM, had been new to another Essex operator, Regal Busways, in 2005. On 1 July 2014 this thirty-seven-seat MCV-bodied Dennis Dart SLF is seen arriving at Lakeside shopping centre's bus station on route 33 from Grays.

Ensignbus service 44 also runs between Lakeside shopping centre and Grays, but travels via Purfleet. Starting out on its journey on 1 July 2014 is number 702 (PX61 AYA), an Alexander Dennis Enviro thirty-eight-seater saloon. It had been new to Wray's of Wigton, who had used it on services in and around Carlisle.

Avro Coaches, also trading as Elm Park, was an operator specialising in contract work around the industrial sites of South Essex. In the depot yard, at Rookery Hill, Corringham, are three vehicles, photographed in 1976. On the left is RUF 205, formerly number 205 in the Southdown fleet. It is a 1957-built Leyland PD2/12 with East Lancs bodywork. Alongside it is an ex-Western SMT Bristol LD6G/ECW, registered JSD 934. On the right is Ford R192/Duple coach RDA 810F, new to Don Everall of Wolverhampton.

PWS 998 in the Avro fleet was an unusual one, as it carried the unique Homalloy front, giving it a rather mournful look. The Leyland PD3/2 had been new to Edinburgh Corporation in 1957, with Alexander seventy-two-seat bodywork. It later passed to Highland Omnibuses, before heading south to Essex. It is seen in a yard off the A13 near Corringham in January 1980.

Amber Coaches, based at Rawreth Industrial Estate in Rayleigh, has been in business for over forty years, but the company has only recently entered the stage-carriage market. Seen in Grays on the 265 route to West Horndon on 1 July 2014 is KU02 YBE, a Dennis Dart SLF bodied by Caetano. This is another bus that had started life with Mitcham Belle.

Brentwood-based Clintona Minicoaches operated a sizeable fleet of small vehicles, some of which were used on local stage-carriage duties. One such bus was BX56 VTE, a Mercedes-Benz Sprinter, seen on route 99 at Tilbury Ferry terminal, where it would have connected with the little boat the regularly crosses the Thames to Gravesend. Service 99 replaced the rail service that previously ran between Tilbury Town and Tilbury Riverside. The photograph was taken on the damp evening of 20 June 2008. Clintona ceased trading in 2012.

Nelson's Independent Bus Services has today shortened it name to just NIBS; both titles are clearly displayed on ATA 767L, seen in Vange, a part of Basildon, on 6 January 1991. The bus is an ex-Western National Bristol RELL6G/ECW fifty-three-seater, which carried fleet number 2767 in its NBC days. (Richard Huggins)

NIBS, with an operating base at Bruce Grove, Wickford, runs several services in that area and into the new town of Basildon. It is there, in February 1997, at the bus station, that we see F616 CWJ. It is a most unusual Neoplan N416 integral vehicle, built in 1988 by Carlton PSV and used by the associated SUT concern in the Sheffield area. SUT later passed to South Yorkshire operator Mainline.

Phoenix Student Travel did exactly what one would expect them to do. Their main function was to ferry schoolchildren around the Chelmsford area. On 7 March 2002, Richard Huggins photographed C94 CHM at Willow Green, Ingatestone. New to London Buses in 1986, when it carried fleet number L94, it is an ECW-bodied Leyland Olympian. Originally dual-doored, it had been converted to H42/30F layout by Ensign's in 1997.

Thames Weald was founded in 1961 by Doctor Herbert Nesbitt Hefferman, operating in Kent. In 1967, a Romford–Sevenoaks service began, using the Dartford Tunnel. Often driven by Doctor Hefferman himself, the services saw many extensions and cutbacks, even more so after deregulation. In spring 1991 Ford Transit minibus H192 EKN was photographed in Southend-on-Sea, heading for Maidstone, though lettering on the outside of the bus stated that the company ran service between Sevenoaks and Cambridge, plus Dartford to Folkestone. The cross-river services finally ceased in 1998.

Town & Country's two-tone blue livery was a common site around South Essex in the early years of the twenty-first century. At Grays in June 2004, ex-London Buses C43 CHM, a Leyland Olympian/ECW, allegedly 'Not in Service'. Given fleet number 208, it had carried L43 when in London service. Town & Country ceased trading in 2006 and the bus later saw further service with Emblings of Guyhirn, Cambridgeshire.

Essex County Bus was a short-lived operation running services around Chelmsford. It had been intended to give the fleet a more jazzy identity, and the public were asked for suggestions – hence the question mark displayed on AE08 DLF. This Alexander Dennis Enviro 200, with MCV thirty-seven-seat bodywork, is seen in Chelmsford, passing the bus station, on 27 January 2010.

Boreham is a village about 6 miles to the east of Chelmsford, now by-passed by the A12 trunk road. It was home to Boon's Coaches, which was established during the Second World War. The company has long been associated with schools, contract and coaching work. At the depot in the spring of 1978 is 579 RKJ, an ex-Maidstone & District Leyland Atlantean PDR1/1, built in 1961 with MCW bodywork. Alongside is SNO 398R, a Bedford VAS5/Plaxton twenty-nine-seat coach, bought new by Boon's in December 1976.

Clearly owned by Boon's of Boreham is SCO 419L, formerly Plymouth City Transport Leyland National number 19. During its life in Devon, it had been dual-doored, with a seating capacity of forty-six, but had been converted to single-door operation when photographed at Boon's Church Road premises in 1981. The depot has since been demolished, making way for Boon's Close.

Fargo Coachlines, based at Rayne near Braintree, have been involved in a small amount of stage-carriage operations. On such duties, at Braintree's small bus station in the summer of 1993 is KHB 35W. This Ford R1114/Plaxton Supreme Express fifty-three-seater had been new to Welsh operator Bebb's of Llantwit Fardre. It is about to depart on service 356 to Tye Green. Vehicles of Hedingham Omnibuses and Eastern National are also seen.

Don's of Great Dunmow is a well-known coach business operating school, contract and private-hire duties. A great variety of interesting buses has been owned over the years. On a dull day in 1982, GNS 668N is seen in the depot yard. New to Greater Glasgow PTE in 1974, it is one of many Leyland Atlantean AN68/1R types that ran in the Scottish city. It carries an Alexander seventy-six-seat body. Don's also had a yard in Bishop's Stortford, just over the border in Hertfordshire.

S&M Coaches, also trading as Castlepoint Bus Company, was a company running many contract services around South Essex. At the firm's cramped depot yard in South Benfleet, *c.* 1975, is RAL 333. This all-Leyland PD2/12 fifty-six-seat bus had been new to Barton Transport in 1954, when it sported fleet number 731.

On the same occasion as above, we see another ex-Barton double-decker, 901 LRR, which was a Barton BTD2 rebuilt, bodied by Northern Counties. The main subject of the photograph, though, is VTX 443. New to Rhondda Transport as number 443 in 1958, it is an AEC Regent V with Weymann seventy-seat forward-entrance bodywork. As can be seen, it carries S&M identification.

On a different occasion, *c.* 1978, at S&M/Castlepoint's South Benfleet depot, we see an ex-Merseyside PTE Leyland Atlantean PDR1/1 with Metro Cammell bodywork. Evidence of the previous owners is clearly visible. HHF 9 had been new in 1960, as number 3 in the Wallasey Corporation Motors fleet.

Much of the S&M/Castlepoint fleet could be found out-stationed at various locations throughout South Essex. WOV 20J is seen at a large transport café car park, near North Benfleet, *c.* 1978. This rare AEC Reliance/Caetano fifty-one-seat coach had been new to Mason of Darlaston, a West Midlands coach operator.

Grey-Green, a famous London-based coach concern, ran some express services to the Essex coast. Therefore the company's coaches could often be found in Colchester bus station, while refreshments were taken. That much-photographed dovecot forms the backdrop to Volvo B58-56/Duple Dominant EYH 804V and CYH 790V, a Bedford YMT, again with a Duple coach body. Taken sometime in 1980, both coaches were almost new.

This coach, 447 GYR, had been new to the Ewer Group, owners of Grey-Green. In that company's ownership, it would have been no stranger to the Essex coast and would have felt at home with Harwich and Dovercourt Coaches, where it was photographed at the depot in 1979. A year earlier, this Leyland Leopard L2/Harrington coach had been noted with Hants & Dorset, painted in full NBC red livery.

Travellers from London to Southend Airport by rail were obliged to alight at Rochford station and complete their journey by bus. Channel Coachways provided the link between the two. The regular performer on this service was 8627 DT, a former Doncaster Corporation AEC Reliance with Roe forty-five-seat bodywork. It had been number 27 in the Doncaster fleet when new in 1961 and had later seen service with Golden Miller in Feltham, prior to moving to Essex. This photograph was taken at Southend Airport, sometime around 1975. A brand-new railway station directly serving Southend Airport opened in 2012.

The quaintly named village of High Easter is home to Lodge's Coaches, a small company that runs an infrequent stage service into Chelmsford. While the bus is laying over in the city, it is often to be found parked around the back of the railway station. At that location, on 25 March 2010, is M73 WYG. This MAN 11.190 with Optare Vecta forty-two-seat bodywork had been new to a Yorkshire operator, Black Prince of Morley.

The historic market town of Saffron Walden is home to Viceroy Coaches. Still in business at the time of writing, the company undertakes a variety of bus and coach work, including a small amount of stage-carriage operation. Back in 1974, the depot housed a wonderful collection of vehicles, including a pair of 1949 AEC Regent III 'deckers, new to Pest Control of Cambridge for non-PSV duties. One of these, HER 27, with Weymann fifty-six-seat bodywork, is seen, alongside the sister bus and a fine AEC Matador towing vehicle.

Another visit to Viceroy's premises, sometime around 1977, found that the fleet had been modernised. Several buses had been purchased from Nottingham City Transport, including DAU 370C, seen here. This AEC Renown with Weymann seventy-seat bodywork had been new as NCT number 370 in 1965.

'Picture-postcard' is often the phrase used to describe Finchingfield, situated between Thaxted and the Hedinghams. Wiffen's Coaches were based in the village, but this photograph of 505 DKT was taken in 1977 at the site of Takeley station, on the former Bishop's Stortford–Braintree railway line. The bus was new to Maidstone & District as number DH505 in 1959. It is a Leyland Atlantean PDR1/1 with Metro-Cammell seventy-eight-seat bodywork.

In the early years of the twenty-first century, the Transit Group had become quite large, with operations in Hertfordshire and Essex. The operations in the latter county were branded as Stansted Transit. New to those operations was KE53 VDP, a Transbus Dart SLF, with Transbus twenty-nine-seat bodywork. It is seen in Braintree bus station on 9 May 2007.

Another Stansted Transit vehicle is seen in Chelmsford on 10 May 2007. This 1999-built Optare Metrorider, registered V237 LWU, was capable of carrying thirty-one seated passengers. It had been new to Black Prince, of Morley, West Yorkshire.

Stephensons, based at Rochford, near Southend, have expanded greatly over recent years and the company's vehicles can be found operating services around various parts of Essex and Suffolk. In Maldon town centre, on 19 July 2007, we see fleet number 892 (C92 CHM). This ECW-bodied Leyland Olympian had been new to London Buses in 1986 as L92, fitted with a dual-doorway layout. For use outside the capital it had been converted to H42/30F configuration.

The 61 local circular service in Southend-on-Sea is operated by Stephensons, and fleet number 411 (SK02 XG0) carries dedicated lettering for the route. New to Scottish operator HAD Coaches of Shotts, this Dennis Dart SLF, with a Plaxton twenty-nine-seat body, is seen in Southend on 24 February 2011.

The smart Stephensons fleet contains several buses bought new by the company. One example is number 461 (EU60 CBF). This Alexander Dennis Enviro 2000 with bodywork by the same company, seating thirty-seven, is seen leaving Chelmsford's new bus station for Ongar on 9 September 2010, only a few days after delivery.

New Horizon Travel, trading as Horizon Bus, is a relative newcomer to the independent bus scene in Essex. Based in the village of Frating, the company has run various services around Colchester and Clacton-on-Sea. In the centre of the latter town we see RX51 FNS on 24 October 2013. This Dennis Dart SLF, with Plaxton bodywork, started life with London operator Armchair Passenger Transport.

X974 CNO is the Horizon Bus fleet is an unusual vehicle, in that it was purchased from Irish operator Dublin Bus. It was originally registered 00-D-70021 and given its new identity when it came across the water, hence the Essex registration. This Volvo B6BLE/Wright saloon is seen in Colchester on 13 October 2011.

Another newish Essex bus operator is Regal Busways, which started out in 2001 from its headquarters in Chelmsford. Opposite the bus station there is number 1404 (V764 HBY), a Plaxton-bodied Dennis Trident, which had been new to London operator Metroline as number TP64 in 1999. Photographed on 22 May 2014.

One of Regal Busways' services is branded as the Essex Pullman – route number 1 between Chelmsford and Canvey Island. Three specially liveried Optare Tempo saloons were purchased new for this operation in 2007, though one has since been destroyed by fire. Number PO3 (YJ56 WVY), a thirty-six-seater, is seen in Duke Street, Chelmsford, on 10 May 2007.

Over the years, several double-deckers have lost encounters with Duke Street's railway station bridge in Chelmsford. With care, though, single-deck buses are able to pass through, as proved by Regal Busways' number 801 (RG09 BUS) on 25 March 2010. New to the company in 2009, it is a MAN saloon with Wright forty-four-seat bodywork.

Regal Busways' route 14 runs between Chelmsford and Wickford. On 10 May 2007, number 601 in the fleet is setting out on its journey and is picking up outside the excellent Railway Tavern, close to Chelmsford station. Registered YN04 PZY, it is a Dennis Dart SLF, bodied by Alexander to Plaxton's Pointer design and bought new by Regal Busways in 2004.

Imperial Bus Company was another post-deregulation operator that provided bus services throughout much of Essex between the years of 1991 and 2014, when it ceased trading. Number DL181 in London style, R181 VLA is a thirty-five-seat Dennis Dart/Plaxton saloon, new to Metroline of London. It is seen taking a rest in Chelmsford bus station, prior to operating a service to Ongar on 19 July 2007.

Imperial's R710 MEW did not appear to carry a fleet number when photographed in Chelmsford bus station 27 January 2010. This 1998-built Dennis Dart SLF, with a Marshall thirty-two-seat body, had been new to MTL London Northern.

Since deregulation, the new town of Harlow has seen a rise in the number of independent operators running both tendered and competitive services in the town. One of the first was The Buzz Co-operative, set up in 1988, with a fleet of minibuses running around the estates. The company finally ceased trading in 2003. In February of that year, R108 VLX was photographed at Harlow Town railway station. New to London operator Centrewest, this is a rare example of a Marshall Minibus twenty-six-seater, one of a type that did not find favour with too many operators.

The buses of Centrebus, from across the border in Hertfordshire (though the company is based in Leicester), can be found in Harlow, as a depot has been purchased in the town and some services operated. Departing from the bus station on 8 August 2012 is fleet number 563 (Y352 FJN). Originally built as a dual-door bus, this Dennis Dart SLF, with Alexander bodywork, had been new to the capital's East London operation.

The story of Stansted-based Excel is rather a complicated one. It commenced as part of the Stephenson's of Rochford business in 2003, becoming part of the TGM Group (itself owned by Arriva) in 2008. The main operating area was around Stansted Airport, but L113 YVK was found in Harlow bus station on 28 April 2007. This Northern Counties-bodied Dennis Dart thirty-five-seater had been new to Kentish Bus as number 113 in 1994.

The Optare Alero low-floored minibus never became a great hit with the larger bus companies of the United Kingdom. Nevertheless, over 300 were built, most of them going to local authorities. One such was YN04 XNR, a sixteen-seater, new to North Yorkshire County Council. Seen in the hands of a Harlow operator, LCB Travel, it is seen arriving in the new town's bus station on 8 August 2012.

SM Coaches and its associated Olympian Coaches business run several stage-carriage service around Harlow. Seen laying over in the bus station on 10 August 2010 is OY53 RBU. This rare example of an Irisbus Agora Line integral forty-four-seat saloon had been new to Norfolk County Council, where it had been used on Park & Ride services in Norwich.

Iveco 59.12 minibus M736 AOO, with a twenty-five-seat Marshall body, had been new to Essex-based County Bus in 1995. Still operating in its original area on 28 April 2007, it is seen in Harlow bus station in the hands of Olympian Coaches.